THE
ROMANTASY
COLORING BOOK

THE ROMANTASY
COLORING BOOK

AN ADULT COLORING BOOK
Featuring 24 Gorgeous Romance
& Fantasy-Themed Illustrations

DANIELA LIBERONA

Published by:
Ulysses Press
PO Box 3440
Berkeley, CA 94703
www.ulyssespress.com

ISBN: 978-1-64604-746-8

Page 51: The last coloring page of a soldier being knighted is based on the painting *The Accolade*.

Printed in the United States
2 4 6 8 10 9 7 5 3 1

ABOUT THE ILLUSTRATOR

Daniela Liberona is an illustrator and graphic artist based in Chile.

DISCOVER MORE GREAT COLORING BOOKS
from ULYSSES PRESS

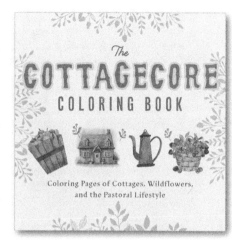

www.ulyssespress.com/coloring

Made in the USA
Las Vegas, NV
22 May 2024